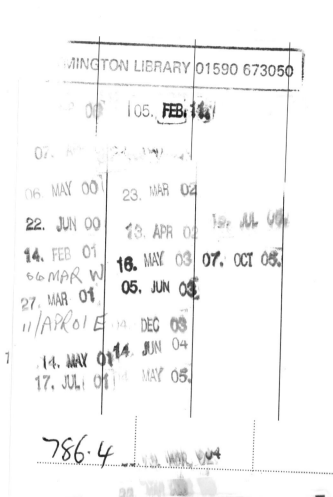

PIANO ADAGIOS

HTK

Selected by Stephen Duro

CHESTER MUSIC
(A division of Music Sales Limited)
8/9 Frith Street
London W1V 5TZ

CONTENTS

This book © Copyright 1999 Chester Music
Order No. CH61572   ISBN 0-7119-7633-3

Cover design by Chloë Alexander
Printed in the United Kingdom by
Caligraving Limited, Thetford, Norfolk

SONATA NO. 22 IN E

Second movement

Franz Joseph Haydn

SONATA NO.6 IN G

Third movement

Franz Joseph Haydn

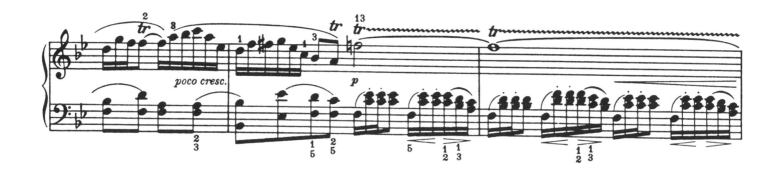

SONATA NO.23 IN F

Second movement

Franz Joseph Haydn

SONATINA IN C
Op.36 No.1

Muzio Clementi

SONATA IN B FLAT MAJOR K.570

Second movement

Wolfgang Amadeus Mozart

SONATA IN C MAJOR K.545

Second movement

Wolfgang Amadeus Mozart

16

SONATA IN G MAJOR OP.79

Second movement

Ludwig van Beethoven

MOONLIGHT SONATA IN C SHARP MINOR

First movement

Ludwig van Beethoven

23

PATHÉTIQUE SONATA IN C MINOR

Second movement

Ludwig van Beethoven

Adagio cantabile ♪ = c.60

NOCTURNE NO.15 IN D MINOR

John Field

NOCTURNE NO.5 IN B FLAT MAJOR

John Field

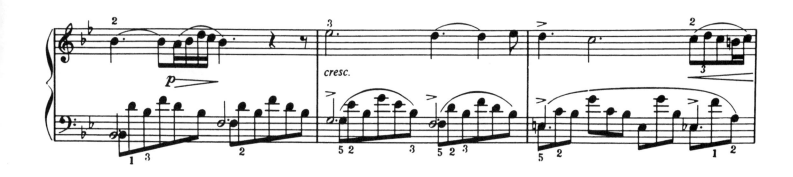
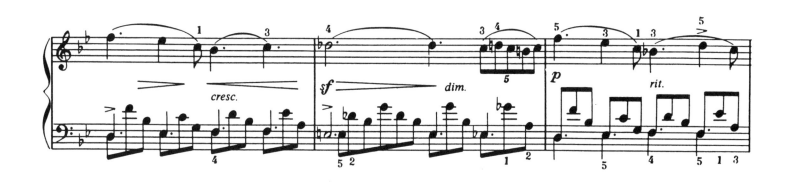
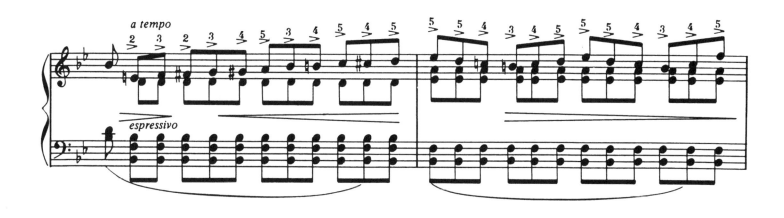
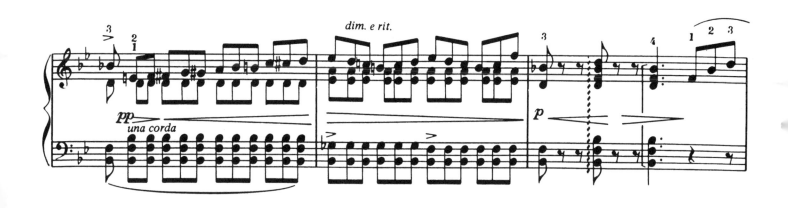

MOMENTS MUSICAUX NO.2 IN A FLAT MAJOR

Op.94/D.780

Franz Schubert

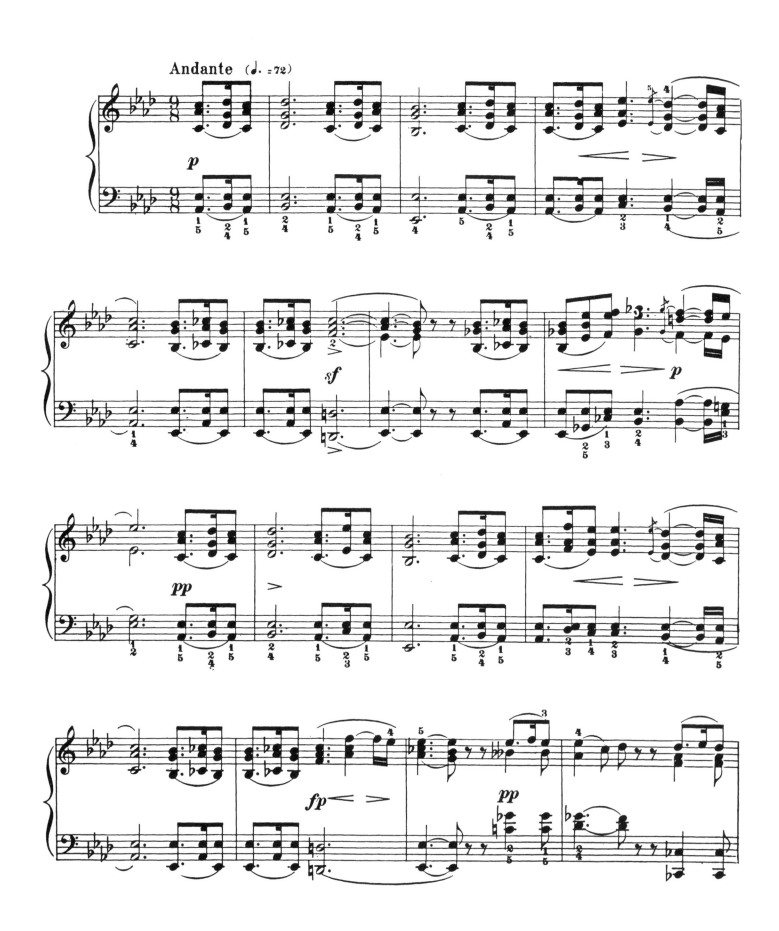

KINDERSTÜCKE NO.2 OP.72

Felix Mendelssohn

REGRETS
Song Without Words No.2 Op.19

Felix Mendelssohn

40

PRELUDE IN B MINOR
Op.28, No.6

Frédéric Chopin

PRELUDE IN E MINOR

Op.28 No.4

Frédéric Chopin

NO.3 WARUM?

from Fantasiestücke Op.12

Robert Schumann

TRÄUMEREI (REVERIE)
from Kinderscenen (Scenes from Childhood)

Robert Schumann

*Original

CONSOLATION NO.4
in D flat major

Franz Liszt

MARCH (SONG OF THE LARK)

No.3 from The Seasons Op.37a

Piotr Ilyich Tchaikovsky

ELEGY
No.7 from Lyric Pieces Op.47

Edvard Grieg

TO A WILD ROSE

from Woodland Sketches Op.51

Edward MacDowell

53

PRELUDE IN D FLAT MAJOR

No.15 Op.11

Alexander Scriabin

Moscow, 1895

1) *rit.*
2) _ _ } according to the composer's instructions.

SONATINA IN G OP.151 NO.1

First movement

Anton Diabelli